'Pile & Plunder'
a form of
Machine Reverse Appliqué

by AbbieAnne Searle

I now understand why some authors have a whole page of thanks!!
I've had so much help and support from so many people it's quite hard for me to get my head around it! So much so that I am just going to issue a blanket
THANK YOU to you all,
you know who you are.

The only exception goes to my long suffering husband Paul, without who's support and huge input to the housework this wouldn't have happened, it's more than appreciated, along with the Yummy Butty's!!!

First published in Great Britain 2011

Text, Artwork & Photography Copyright ©2011 by Abigail Anne Searle
Publisher: AbbieAnne Searle
Written and produced by AbbieAnne Searle

Pictorial Photography by LMJ Photography, Wadebridge, Cornwall
Tutorial Photography by AbbieAnne Searle
Cover Layout inspired by Paul Griffin of Jazz Attack

Computer Technical stuff supported by Bob Wylde of yldonline.com
Printing know-how and general encouragement from Evie Manning of TJ Digital, Padstow, Cornwall

ISBN - 978-0-9570421-0-0

Acknowledgement of support and products used within this publication go to Gutermann for Threads Fiskars for scissors and the general supplying populace of fabrics and sewing items for all manner of useful bits and pieces and fabrics.

Printed by: Peninsular.co.uk
Book Binding by TJ International, Padstow, Cornwall,

CONTENTS

REQUIREMENTS

A desire to have fun and create!!

General sewing supplies
Preferably a sewing machine (although you could do this without)
A selection of fabrics - cottons and whatever else you fancy!
A selection of threads (or just one!!)
A small pair of very sharp scissors!
Pen, paper
Embellishments...........
Time
Warnings to your partner or family who may need to be
prepared to run the risk of not having dinner or housework
done as normal.........

WOT HAPPENED WAS......................

How to get a quick result without a lot of effort? - that was my wonder of the morning whilst showering. There I am having my morning yatter with the plastic turtle that lives in our shower and low and behold, he inspired me!! I won't admit to him actually talking to me, I do quite like my freedom in this world!

Anyway, I decided I quite liked him, apart from his personality, he had some wonderful pattern and shape to him, lots of nice curves and contained areas of colour. I thought silk painting maybe? Gutta and such stuff, but that meant getting all the gear out from behind all the other gear, that was actually behind that part of my 'stash' over there, somewhere in what used to be the spare room......................*I feel sure there are plenty of you out there who will understand this.......*

So, all clean and smelling pretty from the shower, clasping a turtle, off I trundle into the 'unknown' as my husband would have it.....what could I do with this wonderful turtle? I had to do something, he'd been so kind as to inspire me and I really didn't want to do the ironing. A simple drawn pattern would be a good starting point Me thinks. So a line pattern was duly drawn.* It was rubbed out here, scribbled over there and generally faffed with until I had something pleasing to my sense of balance.....Excellent!! Now what though?

Well, there was this really nice piece of batik cotton fabric that had accidently landed within my purchases at Malvern (as things do, along with several other things never declared within the hubby-budget.......)......it was sort of sea-ey, if you sea what I mean?

     sea > water > turtle > swimming > idea!!!!

     So that's the background sorted then!

* you'll find a copy for your use if you want, in the pattern section at the back of the book.

Then I had a more tasteful moment as I dug through my stash for some fabric's that might work. At this point I still hadn't decided what exactly I was going to do to re-produce Mr Turtle, but he was definitely going to be swimming through a batik sea, in tasteful green and turtle-ish fabrics, 'maybe just that little piece there that's not actually cotton, but is rather lovely to feel, that I got to do that bit of embroidery on, well, I think that's what the original intent had been..........'

Then was the problem of technique/style, whatever you would like to refer to it as. 'Do I play bondaweb appliqué? Nah!! That actually involves serious iron usage! Piecing? No, too much like hard work!!' As this type of conversation is going through my mind and to the fabrics in general, (come on, we all do it, we just don't admit to it!!!) I was doodling, white fabric pencil in hand, bit of black cotton fabric nearby, it happens, I can't help myself, turtle ends up drawn in white on black fabric, which is OK, but what do I do with it now?!

At this point, with a silky piece of fabric 'playing' through my fingers, I think of my college tutor who encouraged us to do everything, especially if they said you shouldn't! She had made us do the most hideous lesson in reverse appliqué I could have ever imagined! You try cutting a tear-drop shape through half a dozen layers of satin and sheens, then needle turning each layer under without a 'triffle' amount of fraying!! A lesson imprinted on my mind for which I will be forever grateful Rita!!!   We had such fun in that class, it might be more accurate to have called it a weekly therapy session!

So, reverse appliqué it would be........but I was going to find a way to do this with ease!

Basically.........

In this
book I'm
going to try and
explain to you how
I play with fabrics, on
occasion I've been known to
describe it as 'painting with
fabric'. It really is very easy once
you have sussed the basic method........
layering colour and texture, stitching and shaping.......
whilst adding as much imagination as you would want.
Please enjoy!

Choosing your design.......

To start with I would recommend choosing something simple, that isn't going to be a large overall finish size. Possibly about 12"x12". Try to resist the urge to use a complicated pattern too early on, things can and do, go awry! I generally teach using a 12" square of fabric, the working design is usually well within this area, so maybe that will suit you too? If you're happy with the outcome, you can make good use of this sort of sized panel.

I find it's best to look for a design that is clearly outlined and has defined areas within it. Large-ish areas of colour - sectional such as the turtle's shell. You are going to be working within each small area of the design and will need enough room within each to manoeuvre your scissors.   (Embellishments and added stitching can change this at a later stage if you require smaller detail)

Small area's can be great fun, but are probably not the right thing at the beginning, you stand a chance of putting yourself off from ever using this technique to it's full potential if you start too small.......it can become fiddly and time consuming which is wonderful if that is your thing, but if not, the air surrounding your work area may become a little 'blue'!!

I have included several of my own beginners designs at the back of the book. I generally use these when teaching this technique as a day workshop. Or, you can enjoy designing your own, always so much fun!! I can also recommend children's colouring-in books for inspiration and there are readily available design source books which contain outline drawings covering simple and complicated stuff! *(I like 'stuff!', I think it's a fab word for collectively nice 'things'!!!!)* These type of books are excellent though, for those just starting out or who class themselves as 'unable to draw' (which I totally disagree with, we can all draw something, it's just a line on paper, things do not need to be complicated!)

THOUGHT: If you really are in need of a reason to be playing, this simple start piece when finished can make wonderful embellishments, cushions, pictures, postcards, pin cushions, lampshades, place-mats, brooches, bag & hat adornments, tea cosy's,.............. my list can go on and on, all manner of things fun!

(Be inspired by, but please do be careful not to go around copying other people's designs directly. They may have a copyright on them or may have a design owner who may be offended. My work here has been designed to inspire not to be copied precisely, I'll class it as an honour if this is achieved, the beauty of this technique is that every piece of work should emerge uniquely!!)

So, to start!

This first lesson is designed to be a nice, easy beginning. You should come out with a small, usable motif, ideal for use as an embellishment or as part of a larger appliqué project.

I found one of those little sample swatch packs of fabrics the other day, mostly 4"x4" and very tastefully co-ordinated, you know the ones? - we can't resist them at shows, or have them given to us because we're 'patchers/embroiderer/sewing-Bod's and will know what to do with them', but we don't actually use or need them, we just have them........well they're ideal for this!!!!

As I previously said, simple patterns work well for starters, at least until you get the hang of the basic technique, which really is very basic. It only becomes more difficult if you take the design side of it further as I have, later on in this book. There seems to be no limit to it, I've been playing with it for many years now and still keep finding new stuff to do. I'm also constantly amazed at what other people think to do with it when I'm running workshops.

So when starting out, you should have your simple design and you are preferrably going to use 100% cotton fabrics, it just makes life easier at first. *(They work well layered on each other and have some fraying capabilities without making life a pain.)* I'm sure you've managed a design of your own, but remember, I've put a few in the back of the book for inspiration and quickness..........

I've possibly gone over board with the amount of photos in lesson 1, but my view is, if I can successfully get you all through this first basic project, the rest should be a doddle!

Planning!

Anyone who's ever been to one of my classes will tell you this is where you ought to 'do as I say, not as I do'!

Planning a project is always helpful, not only for a successfully finished item, it often saves time and occasionally money in the long run. I always plan, but I do tend to plan in my head more than I do on paper. I have however, made a huge effort to set a good example throughout the book!..................

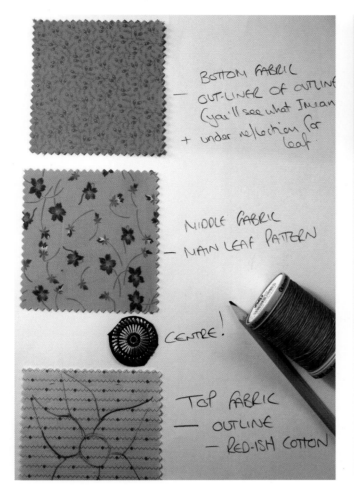

BOTTOM FABRIC
— OUT-LINER OF OUTLINE
(you'll see what I mean
+ under reflection for
leaf.

MIDDLE FABRIC
— MAIN LEAF PATTERN

CENTRE!

TOP FABRIC
— OUTLINE
— RED-ISH COTTON

Scribbled notes, codes, colours or descriptions, any manner of reminder will do so long as you can understand them, even when you return to them at a much later date when the project has become a UFO!!*

It's advisable to keep a note of which areas in the design you intend to display which fabric. We will be piling our fabrics, right-side up on top of each other, then cutting them away to expose the fabrics below. It's very useful to know which fabric will be positioned in which layer for reference as you cut away. Plan your use of colours and thread at this stage as well, the thread will outline the pattern and be seen as an integral part of the finished item.

*UFO – unfinished projects!! I think most of us have a few of these hidden somewhere......

(cups of tea or coffee are always a good thing to have when starting a project, or at any time along the way.......mines a white coffee please, no sugar, not too strong!)

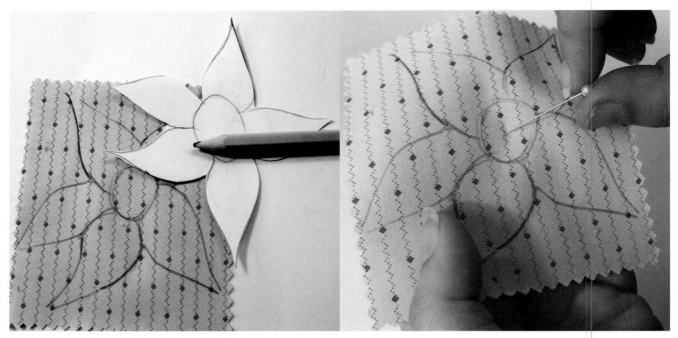

Having drawn your design on thick-ish paper or card, cut it out around it's outside edge, ready to be used as a template.
(I often use off-cuts of mount board from the local picture framer, although it can be a little thick when working small detailed designs, it's well worth looking for unwanted off-cuts)

Now select a fabric for your top outline fabric, it will provide a defining line to your motif. As we will be cutting away most of this fabric, the colour is more important than the design when you're choosing. The fabric that is left will also have a lot of stitching on it covering more of the design and colour. So do not agonize over and then waste your favorite fabric yet, just take into account the overall colour of it.

Place your template in the middle of the top fabric, which should be right-side up and proceed to draw around it. *I tend to use a 2B pencil for just about everything, if that fails to give a visible line on the fabric, I use a white or coloured pastel or chalk pencil/ fabric marker.* You're going to machine stitch over the top of the drawn line, so don't overly worry about it being seen on the finished item......I have been known to use a pen if that's all I can lay my mitts on!

Try to leave at least a half-inch of spare fabric around the outside of the design to allow for any 'design developments'! *('things wot go wrong' or 'unexpected happenings'...........)*

18

In this example I'm going to use a small piece of embroidered trimming as the centre piece of the flower. To enable ease of layering and machining at the next stage, I am going to demonstrate how to make life a little easier when using a specific fabric/motif in one specific place, we do this before the rest of the fabrics are stacked beneath.

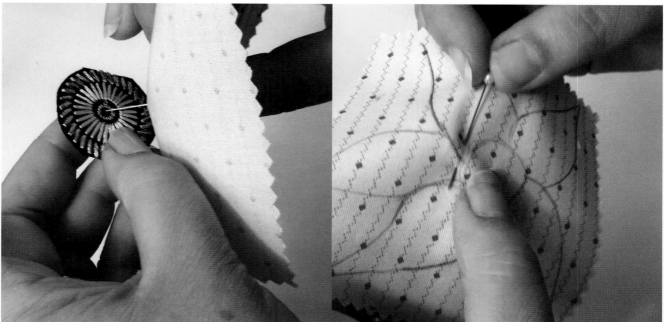

Take the top fabric with the marked design right-side up. Place a pin through the centre of the area where you want to expose the specific fabric, then continue the pin through the centre of the fabric/motif to be exposed, again right-side up. Pin this securely into place from the top so that it will not move significantly when the design is machined through the two layers. *(be careful to pin out of the way of your sewing line, broken machine needles can be annoying!)*

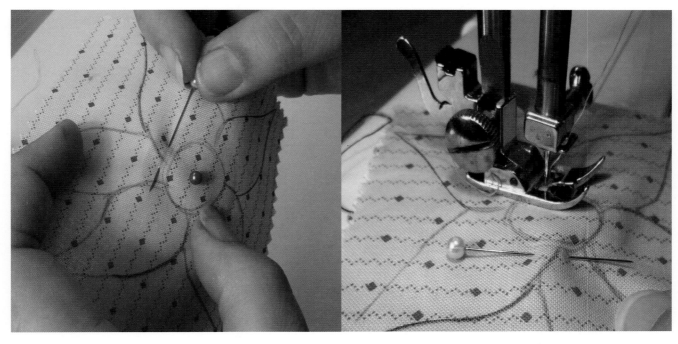

I generally use quite a tight zigzag stitch to machine the layers together. Because the fabric will be cut away to expose raw edges, it's important to use a stitch that will secure the threads in the weave of the fabric, fraying can look wonderful, but we don't really want the motif falling apart! Satin stitch is also wonderful, it gives you a very definite outline.

I have hand-stitched the design through the fabric layers before now, it can be done with some wonderful fancy stitching, but be sure to make the stitches small enough to secure the threads of the fabrics! It can be very time consuming, but if that's what you enjoy, then please go ahead and enjoy!

When the design has been stitched through both of the fabrics, cut away the surplus from the motif underneath, taking care not to cut the top layer of fabric anywhere. This will reduce the bulk within the layering and help to make the cutting away of the other fabrics easier and more accurate later. *(remember, at this stage you should not have cut anything away from the top fabric!)*

Time now to pile up the fabrics, machine in the design and start cutting!!!.................sounds easy eh? Well it is!........

20

Start with the **top layer** showing the design right-side up (with any specifics already attached to it's underneath)

1st layer underneath the design - ought to be the fabric that is going to be exposed the most, it just makes life easier to have to cut through just the one fabric to expose it, it also helps with the accuracy of the design and neatness of the exposed cut edges.

2nd layer - the next most exposed fabric (or bottom layer if you have used only 3) for the same reason, ease of removal of top fabrics and accuracy

3rd layer - the least to be exposed, bottom layer and possibly you might want to exposed it as an outside edging to the motif
(you can keep layering as many as you need or as many as your machine can cope with!)

I generally cut away a little of each fabric at one corner to expose the layers beneath, in the order that they are stacked, just as a reminder of where things are as I work. This can be very important when working larger projects with many layers.

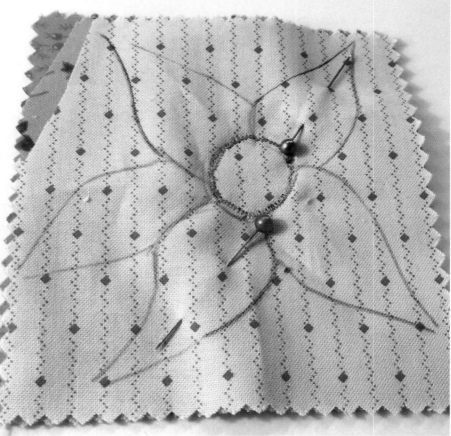

(I also tack through all layers if working on larger projects, smaller ones like this can be well-pinned to achieve a happy finish)

Now, having well-pinned the layers together, it's time to zigzag in the rest of the design though all of the layers.

Remember to tone your threads to your work, they are going to be very visible, variegated threads can work very well, or maybe you want to use different colours around different areas?

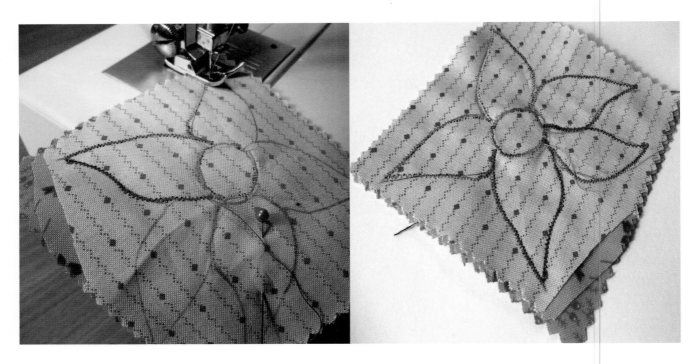

If you're having problems seeing the design line on your top fabric when you're sewing, it can help to have a quick look at the bottom of your project to check what stitching is showing, this can help to ensure you've missed none of the design before you start cutting away. Bits and pieces of design missed at this stage can alter your finished design completely, or cause 'on-going design moments' for your finished item!

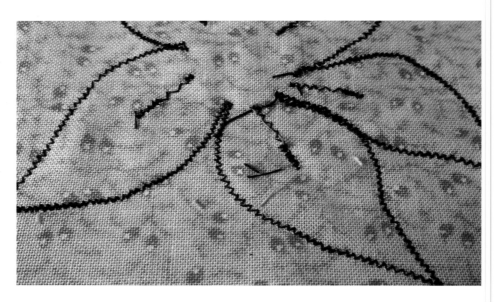

When you are happy that you have all of your design sewn in, it's time to start cutting away fabrics from the top layer down, to expose those beneath.

Do find a small, very sharp pair of scissors that you can use comfortably. *(why do scissors for fine detailed work always have small finger holes??? I have large fingers...........obviously I must have been designed specifically for large detailed work only!!)* Anyway, you need a nice sharp pair of scissors that can get you into tiddly places..........

When practical, I like to start in the middle - wherever you choose to start cutting, please take your time! If you start rushing at this point you can inadvertently cut through too many layers, this makes for rapid changes to your design as you re-calculate what fabric is now going to show where!

So, carefully cut through and take away the top layer to expose the centre detail. You also need to be careful not to cut through the stitching, this could cause your work to unravel at some point in the future. If you do happen to cut through your stitching when you don't mean to, pop it back under the sewing machine and just re-zigzag that small area while it's not too much hassle. Obviously you can do this at any point along the way, stitch it by hand if you need to, just make sure your work isn't going to fall apart!

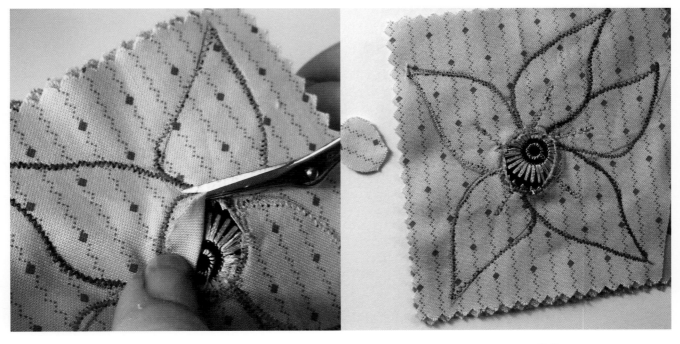

As you can see from the pictures, the centre is slightly off, *(as in, out of alignment, not going green!)* but that's actually how I like things, a little different, not quite perfect. You never know quite what you're going to get with this technique, love it!

You may also have noticed that the design stitching wasn't all that wonderful or accurate *(deliberate on this occasion, honest!!)*, this shows just how versatile this technique is, you don't have to be the world best seamstress to get a professional result.

By the time you have cut away the fabrics and made some lovely raw or frayed edges, the shape will encompass any deviations from the exact! *(good innit?!)* Those of you who are excellent seamstresses, can get very accurate, detailed finishes to some very complicated works...... I have seen this at some of my workshops, quite amazing!

All items produced are lovely though. The mere fact that you have taken the time to make an individual item makes each and everyone special and unique.

Work your way around the design cutting away layers until you have exposed all areas at the level you want. Remember, slowly and carefully to start!!

I like to cut around an area without totally removing it so that you get a bit of a 3D effect - see how the top pink layer is still attached to the middle of the flower? It exposes the darker pink layer below, hopefully giving the impression of petals.

I then like to remove just a sliver of fabric from the egde of top 'petal' to help show just a fraction of what's beneath, all good for effect!

Time now to remove the outside, top fabric, if this is to be a stand alone motif. It might be, that as part of a larger project the top fabric becomes the back-ground fabric of the finished item.

You can now see how the top fabric has become an outline only, by adjusting the width that you leave behind when cutting, you change the overall effect of the design. On this example I have left a little showing on the outside edge to highlight and lighten the overall finish.

I very often use plain fabrics for the outline, more often than not black or a very dark colour, although I've made *(another)* effort to use different colours for the samples within this book. I'm fully aware I like things to be bold and dramatic, where as the majority of the populous prefer subtle and stylish! *(I just can't help myself!!)*

You could leave your motif as finished at this point, the bottom layer attached and showing as a background, or you might prefer to remove that as well?

I have also cut the bottom layer wide of the machined design line, giving another outline to the finished motif. It should now be ready to apply to wherever or whatever you have in mind!

If you love to embellish, now's the time to play. I often embroider or add beads/buttons/ribbons at this stage, whatever takes your fancy - remember, **nothing is ever wrong or right, just maybe not as planned and always a lesson learned!**

Session one as a Visual!.........

Just because I love colour and playing, I'm going to show you a series of photos which follow through another motif, similar to the one in the first section. No explanations and yattering from Me this time. Hopefully you will see the logical stages to this technique when they are shown without 'blurb' in-between.

Please enjoy, I did!

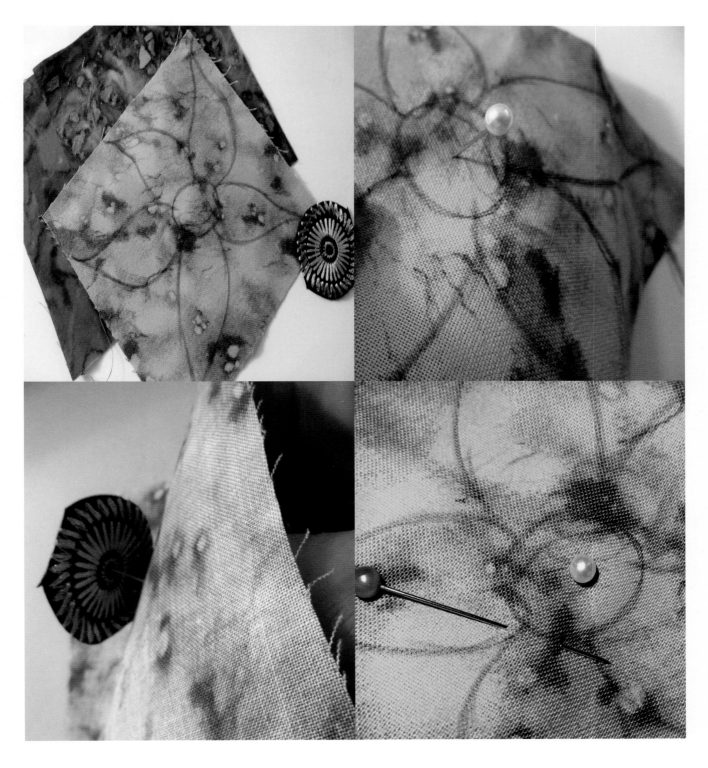

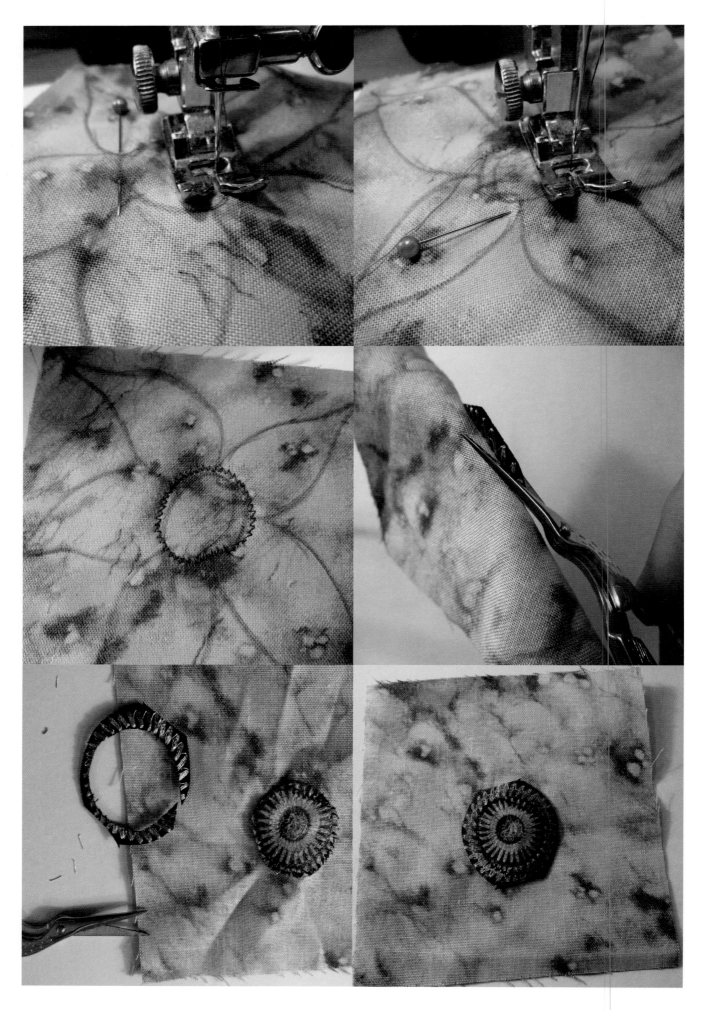

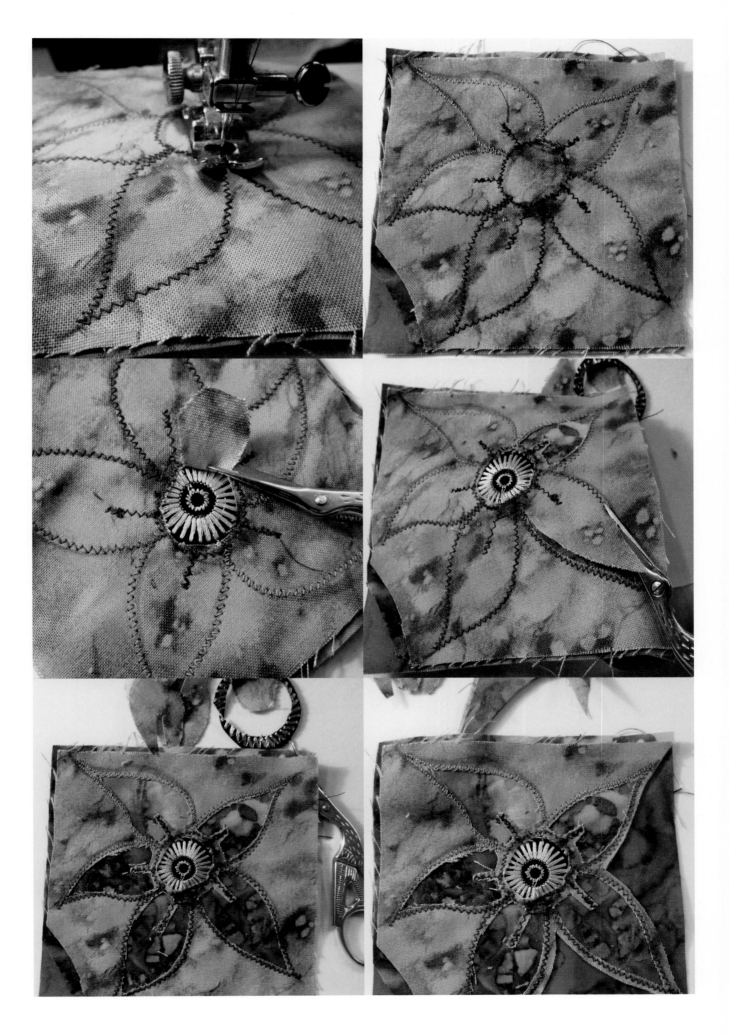

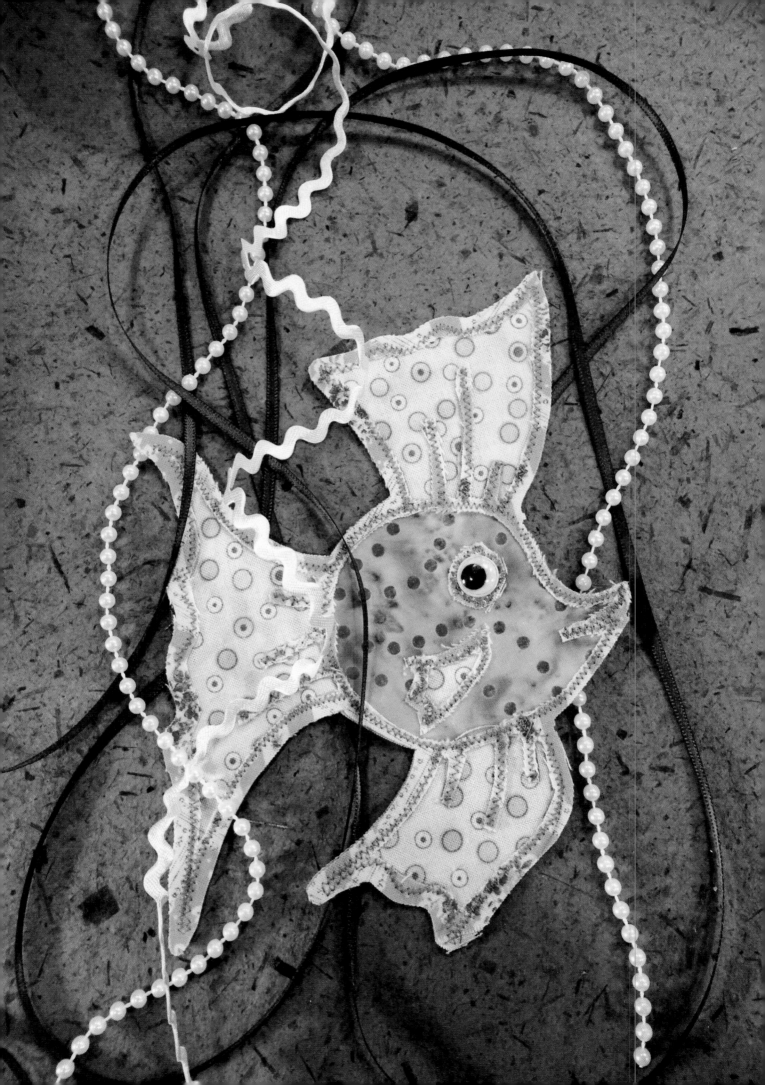

Session One in Brief...............

......as a reminder, or for those of you who prefer things simply stated without major explanations or Me whittering on!!

=> Make a basic template design

=> Draw around this on the right side of the top fabric – leave a little excess around for edging later

=> Pin any specific fabric, right side up, below the area where it's to be exposed. Be mindful to keep pins away from your sewing line

=> Use a fairly tight zigzag or satin stitch to machine the appropriate design above the specific fabric to hold it in place

=> Trim away any excess from the lower fabric

=> Pile the other fabrics below the top design fabric, right sides up, then pin them together ready to machine in the rest of the design from above

=> Machine in the remaining parts of the design through all of the layers of fabric using a zigzag/satin stitch

=> Cut away layers of fabric from within the design area surrounded by stitching to reveal the fabrics below. Be careful not to hurry this part at first as mistakes are easily made

=> Remove the outer edge or maybe leave one of the layers as a background fabric

=> Job done!!

=> Apply your motif where and as intended, hats, brooches, jean's embellishments, quilts, embroideries, it's endless!!!

Although I have given you a real quick basic here, I hope you'll look further into this book, there's so much more stuff to explore, I'll give you as many tips and bits of inspiration as I can, believe me, many years of playing from this simple start has given rise to all manner of things to be aware of!

Stitching & Texture...........

Having covered the basics, I would now like
to take you a little further along the 'Play Line'!

The easiest way to start making differences and enhancements
to your work is through colour and texture. Everybody is capable
of this, it's just a matter of how far you would like to go with it.

I just love to put in some of my stashed fabrics, the little bits of
space dyed velvets, sheers, batiks, all those experiments, dyed and
painted that maybe didn't have the desired outcome at the time!
Bit's of loved clothes and life reminders. I save just about
everything, to my poor husband's horror!!......... *He's evicted me from
the small bedroom as my workroom, to the middle bedroom, until
I started exploding out of that into the living room, he's now put
me up in the loft!! Absolutely brilliant!! So long as I have access to
basic amenities such as coffee and yummy rolls I may never be seen
in the house again!*

This next session will cover another basic design with
some added umph! I'll be skipping some of the very
basic bits that we covered in the first session,
but if you need reminding hopefully a glance
at the photos will do it. I have tried
to cover everything visually if
not in blurb!

37

BUTTONS

FRAMED BLUE EDGE

Remember, the top outline fabric will count as a layer when you are testing the capabilities of your machine. So here I have 5 fabrics ready to layer, I need to remember to add the black fabric for the outline when I test.

Here We go again...........with Heart this time!

Time to choose a design that's a bit more complicated, still sectional within the outer boundaries, so that you can happily 'reveal' sections. *(.....not the seven veils, although I have been known to take classes decorating bras, but that's a whole other story!!.......)*

Remember, you want to be able to use up some of your stash, so lot's of different fabrics! Please run a quick stitch sample with all of the layers you intend using through your machine, before you start final planning. There's nothing worse than having 7 layers in mind and the machine only wants to play with 6!

I find Cotton fabrics tend to work best for the top layer. When you're first starting to use this technique, so long as your item isn't

going to be huge, you may find it easiest to cut all of your fabrics large enough to cover the whole of your design area, except for any individual specifics that you want to attach first, as shown is session one.

You also need to consider how fabrics react to one another when layered and stitched: I tend to put velvets and sheens to the top of the pile when possible, as other fabrics will 'walk' across the top of them on occasion.

Sheers also towards the top. Do test out which fabric you want just below a sheer though, as it will change the appearance and colour of the sheer. *("Audition" your fabrics!)*

It's also worth checking to see if any of the fabrics fray badly, if they do, it might be worth putting them to the bottom of the pile just to save the mess!

Any fabric that is 'heavy' and difficult to cut through may be best toward the top, saves the hands a bit,

Glittery bits and stuff that frays, be aware, you may want to 'place' these before you start the main work, as we did in session one........... (ooooow!........how I love a bit of glit!!)

Also, a slight health warning, if you're using fabrics that have sequins or embellishments already stitched within them, check your machine needle will cope with it and that it won't go breaking at every opportunity!

As you can see above, I've made a pattern template on paper this time. *(photocopies are good)* I then used a yellow marking pencil to draw around the outside edge. I cut away a section at a time and keep drawing around the remaining edges until the whole design is transferred onto the fabric, whittling away as it were! *(Please make sure you use paper scissors for the job, there's nothing I hate more, than fabric scissors used for the wrong purpose! I have different coloured ribbons tied through the handles of my scissors so that I remember which is which, it also serves to identify them as mine and stop other members of the household mistreating them!!)*

I tend to use a plain colour for the top fabric, mostly because it is easier to see what you are drawing, but it also tends to be cheaper and you can change the colouring of it by using different coloured threads.....however, if I have patterned fabrics that are the right colour and maybe need using up for some reason, I'll go with them.

I like to use variegated threads to machine in the design, they help to defuse any hard looking outlines within a piece. You might want to consider using several different threads in different areas of your design.

By changing the style of stitch you can have great fun!! You know all those wonderful looking weird stitches programmed into your sewing machine that you've never had a reason to use? Well, here's your reason!

It doesn't matter if you're a quilter, embroiderer or a
general sewing-bod, play!

Don't forget to practice stitching through your layers before attempting your final piece. Do experiment with the stitch width and length, also the top tension of your machine, as it can give totally different affects through so many layers of fabric. **If you feel the need to touch your bottom tension, please wait! Stop and think first........***if you are experienced with your machine and able to restore it's settings, then go ahead and fiddle. I have a spare bobbin case for my machine that I play around with, I keep* the original one with the factory setting totally separate when I'm messing about, there is nothing more annoying than a bottom tension set wrong, I've known people who have never used their machines again because the original factory setting had been altered and they were unable to restore it.

If you want to use a loose or wide stitch, it might be an idea to machine the design line in with a small straight stitch in the colour of the fabric first. This will hold all the weave of the fabrics together and stop things falling apart! Then go over the top of it in the fancy stitch with a more contrasting colour.

I'm generally boring when it comes to choice of stitch, I tend to use various sizes of zigzag, I know it'll hold things together! I vary the thread type and colour lot's and will use a tiny zigzag or straight stitch in small areas to achieve my visual changes. Metallic threads can be fun. If your machine is a bit temperamental with them, try running them through your bobbin as well as on top, or use as advised by your machine's manufacturer.

When choosing your thread types and colours, do consider which fabric you are going to expose next to which thread.

You might want to use all different colours, it may be better to use the same colour across the whole piece. This will generally give a slight colour change to the whole. Variegated threads mean a nice random finish without all the hassle of re-threading your machine repeatedly.

Do ensure that you have plenty of thread in your bobbin! As you know, it's very annoying to have to stop part way through machining to fill your bobbin, especially when you're using a variegated on the top! It totally disrupts the colour flow!!!
(Don't forget, using zigzag and fancy stitches can use vast amounts of thread! Make sure you have enough before you start.)

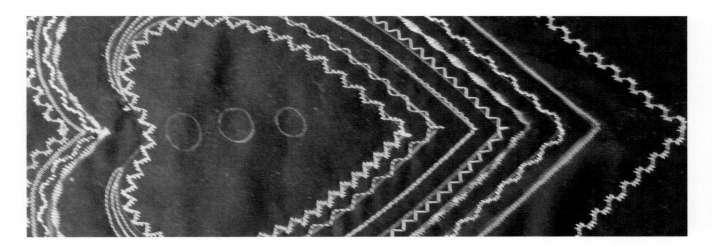

My designs do tend to change as I go along, I have a habit of extending things or varying area sizes as I stitch, if only to cover up deviations of accuracy!! There's nothing wrong with a bit of "on going design development"!

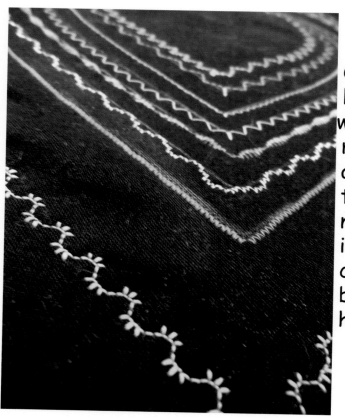

On this first heart, I quite liked what was going happening with the stitching and decided to make things larger by using an added fancy stitch around the outside...............albeit not overly accurately!!......but it'll all come out in the cutting! If it doesn't, I'll be adding some embellishments, hand embroidery or beads..........

Because I like raw edges and rough finishes, I tend to start and finish my stitching using the reverse on my machine. If you prefer not to use this method and would like a tidier finish, leave long enough thread ends to pull through to the back of your work. Do make sure you tie them off well, if you don't, your work may start quietly falling apart!

When machining the design, wherever possible, start your stitching in the middle of the design and work outwards. A bit like quilting, it will help to keep all the layers beneath in line and prevent buckling, although, buckling and creases can look wonderful when the layers above have been cut away, it can help with the textured appearance. These moments are often 'happy accidents' instead of nicely planned designs though!

Thought! - you might want to make notes on your original plan as you go along - stitch type, length, width, tension etc., you have used. It can save time and a minor nightmare at a later date if you need to repeat your work.

Opps!! A wobbly 'design development!..................

Unpickers, a very jolly item that everybody should have!!! We all make mistakes. Unpick if you need to, it will be worth it in the long run! I'm usually happy to have 'free-flow' designs, but here I was running out of room, using a fat fancy stitch right to the top of the design. I unpicked it and used a straight stitch to start at the top, then changed to the fancy oval when I reached

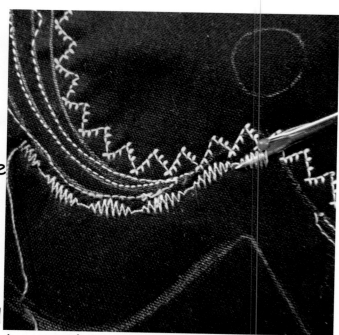

a point where I had enough room to continue around the heart..........................and at that point I felt the need for coffee!!!!

Do take breaks away from your work, having taught workshops of this technique, it seems people can get very engrossed in what they are doing. Regular breaks are important to keep you focused, it stop's eye strain, headaches and swearing!

(Can I also recommend some happy music in the background when working? Nothing quite like a bit of a chair bop and sing along when there's no one else about!!......similar to when we're in the car and the Whitney Houston comes out in us – we know we can reach that high note with no problem................!)

When cutting thin strips away within your design area, it may help to hold the end of the piece being cut away a bit taught. Once you are a little more confident, this tension allows quick working and an even cut from the stitching.

Although you have already planned your design, as the layers are cut away, think about how the width of the remaining top fabric can change, hopefully, enhance the look of your piece. Also, quite often things do not look as expected, or you may just change your mind, but if you re-assess the appearance of your design as you go, you should hopefully have enough time to make changes to it,

I sometimes cut wide of the stitching as I remove layers, as I have in the middle area above. Hopefully the thicker black edge will give extra definition to the centre and show off the first round of fancy stitching better. The second area has then been cut away following the zigzag, this has changed the whole appearance again.

As I've been cutting away areas here, it seems the black fabric within the zigzag cut and plain cream linen fabric, fray quite badly........lot's of little annoying bits all over my work!! I find using picture framing tape to remove them works wonders! Masking tape works quite well, parcel tape is annoying, it doubles up on its self, cello-tape takes forever!

Gradually cut away all the layers within each design area to reveal your pattern. You'll notice I have left a very wide edge around the outside round of stitching, I've then exposed wide areas of the fabric from below for the background.........

'Pinking' edges gives another affect, as does, snipping layers along the edge giving a feathered appearance for the fabric beneath to show through..........

Above I have now gently rubbed the snipped edge to lift it, showing more of the layer beneath.

Below I have placed small beads in the button holes when attaching the buttons, this just gives a slightly different appearance to the work...........time to embellish now if thats what you fancy!!

.... They parked Me in a bush you know!!.....

Traditional Patterns......

.........work wonderfully! But you might not want them for traditional use without a bit of forethought. Remember that when you have cut away the layers you will have raw edges showing all over your quilt. There is nothing wrong with this at all, you just need to be aware you don't want to be washing a cot quilt every 5 minutes, it may well fall apart if the stitching hasn't been done well........

However, if you ensure you use a real close, tight stitch, it can be fairly wide, maybe a satin stitch (or a fancy stitch with a multiple stitch makeup), this will hold the weave of your fabrics together. Your quilt should be perfectly capable of coping with a gentle wash in a machine. What will happen, is that the raw edges, dependant on how close you have cut the fabric to the stitching, will fray a little and soften with wear, not a bad thing at all!

This is my 'Ropey' Quilt!!

I was sat hand quilting this lappy* at work one day, when a couple of customers came into the shop. *(I work in an arts and crafts supply store......heaven!!! Fabrics & threads & paint & stuff everywhere!!)* Anyway, I trundled off to the counter to serve a lady and came back to find a quilter's husband inspecting my work. He was surprisingly knowledgeable, he knew all about log cabins and stuff, quite impressive. He liked my quilt, feeling around the blocks, even inspected my quilting stitch (hand quilting's not the most favourite part of making a quilt for me, far too slow!) and then he asks 'it's a bit ropey here and here isn't it?'........................you would have been very proud of me!! I was polite and everything!! I took great pains to explain that they were in fact raw edges and meant to be like it.................... I do believe he probably prefers traditional quilts!!!

Since this incident which amused my work colleague muchly, this lappy has quite obviously been affectionately known as 'The Ropey Quilt'.

* Lappy – Lap Quilt, technical but in a different way to a laptop computer!!

I am not going to give you specifics as to how to make a quilt, just general guidelines as to how I have incorporated my technique within traditional methods.

Do make a plan showing your chosen design blocks and where your intended use of fabrics will be. Choose your fabrics, making sure you have enough of each to cover the required areas from below. This technique may use more fabric than usual, but it makes up for that by the quickness of completion! It took me just 3 days in-between working and family stuff* to make this lappy, hand quilted even!

Draw out your patterns on your top fabric as usual.

Please practice your stitch though the equivalent amount of layers as you will be using in your quilt blocks. Get the sizing and tension right for the intended usage of your quilt.

*no ironing or vaccing mind!!!!

I find it best to cut all my fabric squares the same size then pile them up beneath each block pattern ready to machine. Be careful not to get too carried away though, remember, you might not be using all of the fabrics in all of the blocks.

I then load several bobbins with appropriate thread so that I don't have to stop and fiddle too much once I've started to stitch my design into place. It takes quite a bit of thread if you are going to use a tight satin stitch.......although in this sample I just used a zigzag, the quilt is for a lappy and won't get masses of use, so continual cleaning shouldn't be a major issue.

Stitch in your design, I've used a variegated thread on this Rose of Shannon block.
I have ensured that the fabric on the bottom of the all of the blocks is the same, this will become my final background fabric to each block. So no cutting the bottom layer through or away!

Now get your lovely little, sharp scissors and start cutting away!!

Make sure all of your blocks are fully cut and your fabrics exposed. This then makes the marking of your outside sewing line on your block much easier, especially those that need to be centred. They're now ready to be joined by sashings, or your preferred method for quilt making.

If you do happen to cut through a layer you hadn't intended to, you can consider changing your design to enable you to expose one of the fabrics below......can you re-stitch that area to cover the hole? If these options are not possible, can you attach another piece of fabric from below to replace the one cut in error? There is always a way to fix it, even if it means appliquéing the whole motif/pattern/block onto a new background!!

Please note that you'll need to put a background fabric on all blocks, even those that normally wouldn't need one, such as the log-cabin showing in the middle-bottom of the picture above. (this prevents too many awkward layers within the joining seams of your quilt)

Now that all of your blocks are ready, you can join them with sashings or in whatever style you want to.......Then you can tack or stick your wadding and backing in place ready to start your quilting.............

Quilt in a pattern of your choice.................can I suggest doing something a bit different from your normal? Maybe use a thick thread, embroidery threads are good.   Possibly several different colours? Maybe use a large running stitch for your quilting? Use a quilting pattern you wouldn't normally? Anything goes, so long as you like it and it holds everything together nicely!

Working a slightly larger project.........

All the basic rules, methods and instructions that I've already described apply, plus here's a few more helpful hints!!

Again I'm going to show lots of developmental pictures, assuming that you have read what's come before, or that the pictures themselves will act as the words of direction........

I have chosen batiks, mixed patterns and shading, no definite repeat patterns though. This fabric mix works for me, in that I find I get a random result when they are exposed. Small patterns can work wonderfully because you'll know what you are likely to uncover in your design. Large repeat patterns work for the same reason as batiks and random patterns, you never know quite what you are going to get. Usually, a more flowing result.

It's your design - play, experiment, use what works for you. Hopefully you'll find that you can transfer your own style of working and design to this technique.

I have also used some glittery net, *(I do love a bit of giltt!!!)* use whatever type of fabric you think will do the job for your design and need. Just remember the affect they may have on each other in both colour and movement between layers.

Stitch in your design, when you get to larger pieces of work, try always to start machining the design from the middle. Remember, it helps to keep the layers flat, helps to stop creasing and buckling and generally makes life easier!

I've used a white pastel pencil to mark out the design on this occasion. I find a paper template best, cut away as you draw around it. Obviously, if you have a different method for transferring your design, all well and good! Happily, the pastel marking lines have all but disappeared by the time I've finished machining.

You can see around the edge of the design that I've allowed the machine lines to extend beyond the design area. I intend putting an oval mount on the finished item and framing it like a picture, so this won't be seen. They will also add extra support to the piece, The thickness of the layers will raise the mount away from the surface of the work and will keep the glass from touching it when framed.

61

Can you see how this design developed as I went?? In the back of my mind I was thinking a few fields of sunflowers at the bottom working up to some sky...... I'm not sure that's what finally happened as I got carried away with the stripy batik as water or sky......... there's a stained glass feel to it as well.......whatever, it reminds me of sunshine! ....I like sunshine, it does all sorts of wonders for people!

Embellishment time!!

I just adore 'stuff'!!! Everyone who knows me is more than aware not to sit still for too long, I can find a use for all manner of adornments.......clothing fabrics, jewellery, bits of bags............. I've actually noticed on more than one occasion, when I've mentioned that I like someone's item of clothing or the fabric it's made from, they've checked the backs of their skirt on the way out of the door!!! ....one day I shall not disappoint them!! *(if they are lucky, I will have used pinking shears!........it's also possibly just as well I rarely use public transport, all those unsuspecting folk!)*

So feel free to adorn your design, little or lot's, whatever feels good to you!! Of course, embroidery, beads, buttons and bells, sequins, mirrors, ribbons, braiding, yarns, are all good and need little mentioning! Anything goes so long as you like it!! Ear-rings, bits of necklaces and chains work really well!

On this one I felt the need to crystallize it! Hopefully it's given a feel of water to it...........

I've also used a 'loopy' gold braid that I found in the Christmas stash, and some gold bobble-type chain stuff! *(I'm sure there will be a proper name for it, but it can be bought by the metre in amongst ribbons, braids and such)* I've also put a small row of blue seed beads across one area that looked a little plain to me!

Do be careful with your cutting when you're using nets or sheers. I find it works best to expose them first, when I'm concentrating, before I start getting carried away wanting to see the finished result and making a bodge of things! If you do snip through one or two threads of net, you can usually rescue it by tucking it back in place carefully or putting a tiny stitch in an appropriate thread to hold it back in place. It's probably not too crucial if you are making a picture or wall hanging, if however, it is part of a quilt or item that will be washed, do make sure it is very secure, or immediately change your design to avoid disappoint-ment further down the line.

'Sunshine Stuff!'

Bigger moments!!........

Bigger-er projects, large art-quilt projects and stuff that generally needs a bit more thinking about!

Again, I don't intend going over all the basics, but will instead be adding to what we have already done. I will try and explain my thought processes and reasoning for doing stuff throughout this section, however, your way of working may and probably should lead you to do things differently to suit yourself.

Planning!!

I cannot stress enough the need to plan as projects get larger. Things will no doubt change as you go along, but you really need to plan your project as fully as possible, if only to ensure you have enough of the right fabrics and threads to finish the job!

I tend to get sudden inspiration from just about anything. It could be a photo or painting, a view or just one of my doodles. I just love doodling, you never know what's going to emerge. I also find it's a great way of concentrating on something totally different..........*my teachers and course tutors became used to me apparently taking no notice of them whatsoever whilst producing anything up to an A3 sized doodle........I find it helps, we're all different which is a very good thing to my way of thinking*

So, having decided on your overall design, draw it out, play with it, sectionise it. Remember we want areas of colour to work to. I then like to pencil or paint in some colours and shapes, adding colour can totally change your thoughts on the design as a whole.

When you have something pleasing to you, then is the time to stop and think how can I achieve a satisfactory look and feel to my piece. *('piece' – masterpiece for that is what you are going to produce!!)*

I start by dividing up the whole design into sections that are manageable. I originally tried working pieces as a whole up to 3'x5', it can get messy, although it can be done. *(It's no worse than trying to machine-quilt the middle of a large quilt, with a small machine!)*

Anyway, divide your overall design up into sections that appear to you to make sense. You might be thinking one area should be all shades of one colour, where another needs to be completely different, *ie: a landscape may easily be divided into sky area, land mass and water.* It might be that you divide it by texture and the types of materials you need to use within an area. Or it may depend upon materials available, perhaps you have just a little of the most fabulous fabric and need to make the most of it, in which case do the best bits first!

Make many notes! Clear notes that you will understand in what could be the distant future!

Audition your fabrics, your threads, your embellishments, then all of your fabrics again!! I bet you've more than enough in stashes, but probably you'll want to add a few new specifics! Remember, use any type of fabric you want to!! Cottons are lovely, but become limiting when searching for texture and effects.

(.......yes, that is one of my old bras you spy! The iron upholstery made a successful bid for freedom at a young age and I couldn't bring myself to throw it away, I will hurriedly add, it has been laundered!!)

Do make sure you have enough copies of your pattern.

I like to have two full sized patterns. One that I can cut up and another to keep and lay completed sections over as I go. This is so that I can see how well I'm doing and how the over all look of the piece is progressing. I also keep two small copies, one that I can write all over with ease and one that I can save for posterity and for when I loose the original!!

So choose a section to start with. I tend to start with the exciting bits for no particular reason, childish I know, but always fun! With me, it tends to be the brightest bits first, which also happens to be the bits that will dominate and anchor the whole design. The colours in these areas will demand respect from those areas surrounding, which will be made to tone, blend and enhance them.

Although I do try to plan which colours and fabrics go where, as ever, my plans are apt to change as I go along. It might be that I really got it wrong working the types of fabrics together, or the colour balance might go astray. Design Development!!

70

Don't be afraid to change the design as you go if needs be, make small samples of things before making them final. Good ideas rushed can be bad dreams made. But do dare to change things, play with colours and texture until it is right for you. We all see things differently, if you are happy with it and like it, then that is wonderful!

So no surprises that I'm going to start with a flower centre!!

I am going to use a lush ribbed velvet of varying reds.......
A purple and a lilac scrunchy rayon fabric........
Pink silk organza, my multi-coloured/pink lacy bra.......
and what will become the predominant green background fabric.......
A pale pink poly cotton and maybe a purple voile........
The pattern has been chopped out ready to go!

As described before, I then transfer the pattern to the top fabric by drawing around the paper pattern and cutting away sections, then drawing around a bit more, until all the pattern is transferred. Having tried many standard methods to transfer my designs, I still find this is the fastest, easiest method for this particular technique. A cotton or poly-cotton fabric will work best for the top layer, if only because it does take the pattern lines easily compared to other types of fabric.

I have piled the fabrics in the following order ready to plunder:

Green cotton top/1st layer – because it takes the pattern well and will be used as the top layer on all of the sections of the quilt, the colour tying all the sections together .

Red Velvet 2nd layer – because it is so thick and stretchy, it may 'walk' between the layers. As it may vary in colour, I will also be able see what is revealed before I cut away anything else, if I don't like what is developing colour-wise with the design I can safely remove it knowing I have several other fabrics beneath to choose from.

Multicoloured lace 3rd layer – I would normally have had this showing in specific spots and used the technique in the beginning of the book to place it before continuing with the layers. However, on this occasion I haven't as I didn't like the way the red velvet showed through the lace, I did however ensure I had it very well pinned and then tacked into position before I machined the design.

Pink Silk Organza 4th layer – because it looks gorgeous under the lace!   I also didn't have masses of it, so had to be careful to put it where I needed it, the tacking also held this in place.

Lilac scrunched fabric 5th layer – to ensure a good colour contrast was available at the first opportunity within the layers.

Light purple strange feeling voile! 6th layer – I added this one before I stitched, just because I found it in the stash and liked the colour and texture, it's actually quite hard to the touch!

Purple scrunchy fabric 7th layer – This layer is a good colour and more as a stand by in case I get everything wrong or cut through too many layers! (It shows as dark purple on the reverse)

Thread for design outline – as you can easily see from the reverse of the machined design, I have used a fairly thick variegated thread, in pinks so that it tones with the overall colour of the flower, at the same time it will cover some, and tone down the green of the top layer.

At this point in my Saturday morning proceedings, my husband arrived at the top of the stairs with sustenance!! Mmmmmmm! What I hadn't realised was that it was well into Saturday afternoon and he was feeling a bit guilty having been watching the F1 * Qualifying while I worked! I really didn't mind, my coffee had an egg and everything!! He's really very good and does wonders with a hoover as well as a grill & frying pan!! Like so many of us I work and so doing my quilting thing is an extra that gets squeezed in around and about, hence I don't do housework unless I have to! That and I really don't like doing it, a waste of good creativity time I feel!

Refreshed and with a lively tune blasting to help with the chair dancing, I continue!..........

As you can see from the photo before the egg and yummy butty, I have sewn in my design and have cut away all of the excess fabric around the design from beneath, leaving just the top layer that I want to use as a leaf design edging the flower. I have then machined the leaf design through just the top layer of fabric in a green variegated thread. This will become thin and floppy as it will have little support when cut around, hopefully adding a sense of movement and depth to the edge of the flower.

* Formula 1 Racing

74

Now that I have the whole design held with tight stitching, I am happy to begin cutting away the layers to expose the fabrics and colours beneath.

You can see that I have focused on the red velvet first, it's colour changes and could therefore affect the rest of the fabrics to be exposed. By revealing it first I can decide which other fabrics will work next to each shade of red.

Remember – slowly but surely with the cutting!!

Fully cut, I feel there will come a time when I will have to embellish this flower!! It's far too tame for me! Although the dark red areas are lush, they lack a depth, so beads and stuff it will be!

The green edge has become distorted a little which has added to the movement of the leaves. As I like the look of them raised, when it comes time to appliqué the flower into place on the quilt, I will probably raise the flower away from the surface so that

75

The leaves are free floating if you get my meaning?..........

...........and the beads have arrived!!

pearls holding down the net.........

beads nestling into the edge of the cut layers.

I tend to work each detachable area of the design in the same manner *(areas that I will appliqué to the quilt top when it is finished)*. Take your time. Consider how the fabrics of each section look together when they are put into place. It may well be that you produce a section that you think really doesn't work, so do it again! Don't throw the original, it can be used as a motif in something completely different! None should be wasted! I ended up with a whole heap of flowers, not all of them are on the quilt. *(however there's no excuse for me really, I just got carried away!)*

One of the flowers ended up as a rather spectacular embellishment on one of my hand felted bags,

And another sample attached it's self to my sewing basket! *(Both bags have simply had the embellishment sewn onto them)*

The big leafy areas..........

I have chosen mostly cottons for the leaf areas, but only because they have the colours and patterns that I feel I am going to need. There is a lovely lime green linen in there and a fabulous batik that really stretches the imagination when it comes to the colour of leaves. I will also add different fabrics as I go to obtain shading and texture in some places.

I will start to introduce machine embroidery techniques into the mix with the leaves, I want to show shaded areas, colour variations and pattern detail in stitch. The main outline of the first leaf design has been stitched in a fairly loose zigzag, using a light variegated green thread. I will happily use any thread if it goes through my machine, it need only be the right colour and thickness to give the visual impact that I'm looking for. Experiment!!   If you really want to use a specific thread that is playing up in your machine, try marking your design outline on the bottom fabric and using the top thread in your bobbin, it has been known to work..........
(all things reversed and worse around Me!!)

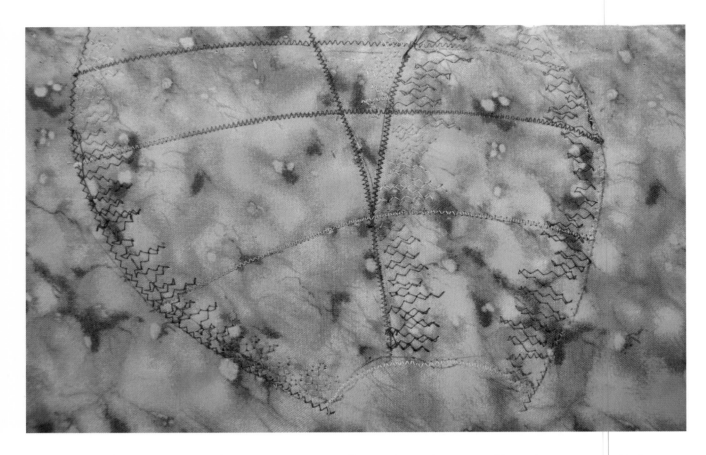

I was able to use a loose zigzag for the design line here, as I knew I was intending to surface stitch through all the layers as well. This would add strength and trap the individual threads of the fabrics stopping the item falling to pieces.

I have then continued to zigzag backwards and forwards across some areas of the leaf that I want to show as a variation of the top fabric. I am guilty of machine abuse at this point! I tend to get carried away at a rate of knots with the feed-dogs up and pull the fabric at angles through the machine, it stops the machining looking regimental, but can totally wreck your machine! I would however suggest that you use a safer method by following the 'free-motion' embroidery instructions for your machine.

This is when I tend to refer to my work as 'painting with fabrics'...... I will cut away some of the layers leaving different widths from the stitching, fray it, zigzagging on it again, changing the thread colours that I am using, cutting a bit more away, maybe changing the stitch size as I go (you could change the stitch type if that is your fancy). I will stitch over and over from different angles, whatever it takes to create a surface that is pleasing.

I tend to follow areas that would be shaded within a picture, trying to replicate the actual, changing the colours where they would normally be seen to change, adding texture through fabric and stitch and later by embellishment or hand stitching/embroidery if it is appropriate. Experiment.

Fray the edges!!........do mind your fingers with these wire brushes, they are lethal!!   *(£1-ish from the local tool shop, they actually come without any oil or rust on them and remain so, as long as you don't let your DIY or car enthusiasts anywhere near them!)*

I found some lovely soft green valour-type fabric, it reminded me of those leaves that have very fine 'hairs' that you can stroke. I have removed the top fabric back to the design line, then cut the next fabric back but not quite as far, I then re-zigzaged over the fabric, snipped into the layers at some points then frayed the edges! Basically I messed about with it a bit, do whatever you think will give you the result you want.

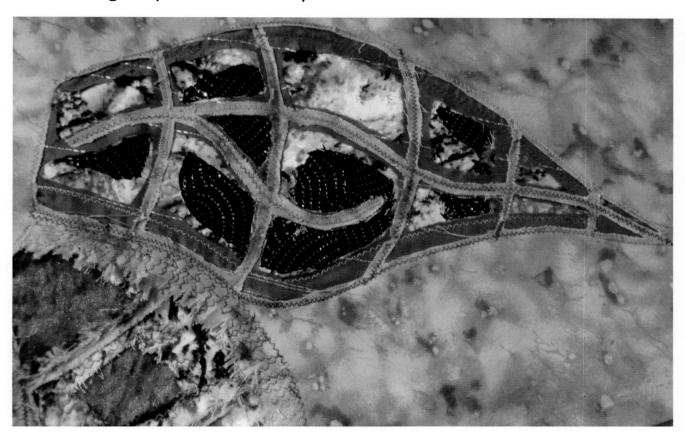

Remember, if at any point it looks like something is going to fall apart, you can always re-stitch it. If its more appropriate, you can stitch another layer of fabric underneath for support, or even add some to the top, it might even look better for it!! In the same vane, if you don't like the look of something you have created, you can always overlay an extra piece of fabric, a bit like using gesso when you're painting!

I am going to be working each leaf area individually, however they all remain attached by the top layer of fabric which is acting as the overall design line and will hopefully be the background as well. Every time I finish an area I place the flower centres and pattern on the top of the fabrics to ensure it still looks as intended.......

I've also added some sari-silks, a glittery black velvet *(gotta have a bit of glit!!!)* another lime linen that's patterned and a glittery Christmas fabric, originally intended for a Christmas tree!!

Play!

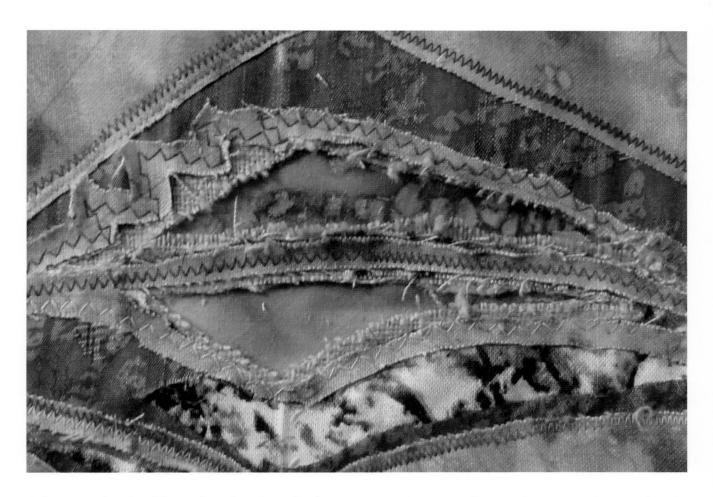

If you don't like the look of the raw edges, of maybe you just don't want quite so many of them, you could satin stitch over some of them to hold them down, add definition, colour and a whole new meaning to things!

Hopefully you can see in the next photo where I have hidden machine stitching beneath a layer of the cut fabric. This is purposefully through the layer of loose woven linen, this should hold things together when I slit and fray it with the metal brush.

Using the brush has a very similar affect to when you would use it in 'cutting and slashing',* it roughs up the edge into a nice soft fuzz........

*(When 'cutting & slashing' I find it better than snipping the fabric edges and then washing it to create a soft frayed edge, its much quicker, removes all the little bits of cut thread and produces a softer finish, just make sure you do it outside on a nice day! In the spring is good, the birds love the fluff for their nests)

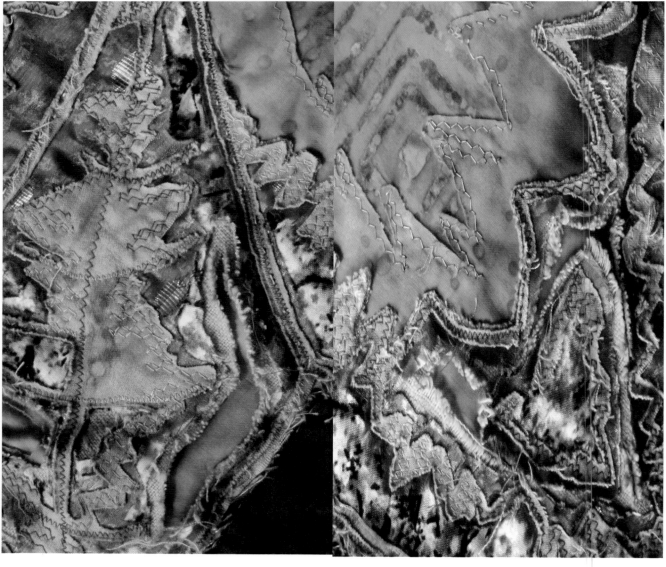

The back doesn't look anywhere near as pretty as the front!! But see how I've trimmed away all of the surplus fabric from around each leaf area underneath. **before** moving onto the next leaf? It's very important as it removes the bulk of unwanted fabric, reduces distortions on the front and lets your quilt/wall-hanging hang correctly when finished. It also stops you trying to put a double amount of layers under your machine needle!

Did I mention, that I generally use a quilting needle in my machine?

It seems to cope with the layers well, but do change whatever needle you choose often for best results, blunt needles cause all manner of problems...... .....look what can happen when you least expect it .... so now to show you some Design Developments!

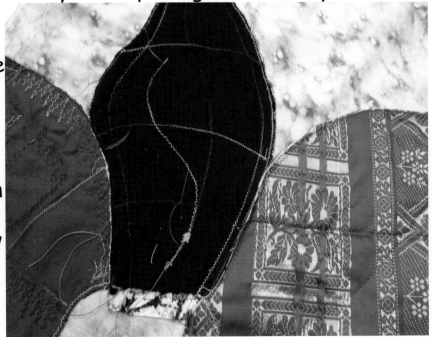

The lovely thick velvet ruckled up between the layers!! Even after I'd put it purposefully as the first layer to try and stop this happening!   But then, everything for a reason. This has actually turned into a happy accident!! It's given height to the flower, allowed more reason for embellishment and basically, I like it!! If it hadn't been the first layer beneath, it would have distorted all of the fabrics above it, and it really wouldn't have looked good. *(maybe had I changed my needle before sewing this section it wouldn't have happened though?)*

The lace looks good too. Where I didn't have very big pieces of fabric *(having vandalised my bra)* I placed a piece to cover the middle section of a flower. Where it has been exposed it has 'run out' towards the edge of the flower, it sits loosely on the fabric beneath. Originally I was just going to cut it away to expose the whole area as the fabric beneath, but instead I've cut the excess netting and partial lace flower away. When I embellish things later I'll put a tiny stitch through the net to hold it in place.........another happy accident!!

(I was once told never to admit to mistakes or errors, always class them as 'by design'.........however you want to look at it, I generally like the outcome!!)

A bit of hand stitching to enhance life!

There's hand stitching on the centre of those flowers and on some of the petals. Notice how I've cut around the edge of the purple sections, but haven't removed the piece totally, just exposing some of the fabric below. I've disguised the machine stitching in the middle of each of the petals by sewing over it by hand with a multi-coloured pearl thread.

I've even used French Knots on the clematis looking flower below! Added a few gold embroidery beads and away we go!!

There really is no limit as to what you can do with this. Please bring your own style and favourite techniques to it. Small, neat and delicate works just as well as my bold and brash!.

Felts can look great! It works really well as a top layer once you have a way to transfer your design line onto it. *(tailors chalk)* There's no frayed edges, sews easily by hand or machine. It can be really cute on toys and kids stuff!   Talking of which, this technique used with a simple pattern on felt can be a marvellous way to introduce kids to sewing with a bit of a difference.

92

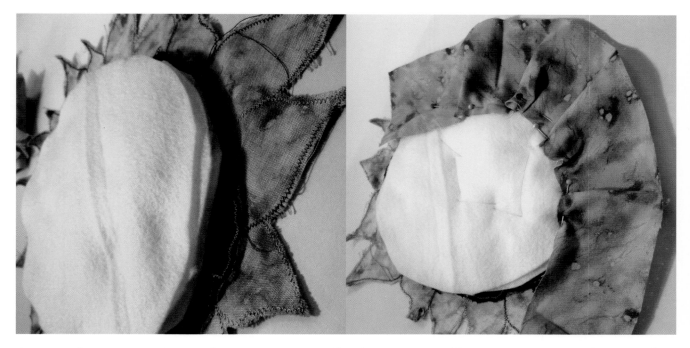

In order to raise the centre of the main flowers away from the quilt top, I've added several layers of wadding beneath them. However, because the wadding would then be showing if the finished wall-hanging was viewed from the side, I needed to ensure it was covered. So I attached a strip of the same green fabric around the outside edge, underneath the flower, right-side showing to the bottom. I then re-stitched the leaf design through the bottom and top layers. I quickly tacked the loose edge in the middle through the wadding to hold every thing in place and then cut away the outer edge of the fabric along the leaf design line. This actually gave the leaves an extra layer of fabric and a bit more stability which was an added bonus! The flower was then ready to be appliquéed to the main body of the quilt when finished.

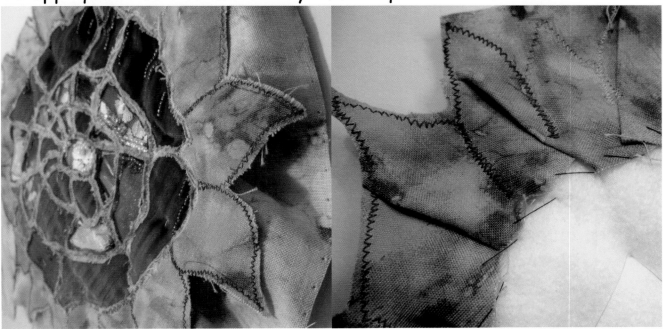

As things progressed with this quilt, it seemed to me that my original plan of using the mottled lime green fabric as the design line and the background wasn't going to work! Things were starting to loose definition. So I decided that when I had completed all the sections I would cut the green away from the outside edge and find a better colour to appliqué the whole lot onto!

As we all know, things like that are sometimes easier said than done! Thus began my search for a replacement background fabric....... we've probably all done something similar even if we don't like to admit it. The classic example is when we've not bought enough of a fabric to finish a quilt because we changed the design half way through, or it was a bit of fabric we just loved and bought on a whim then couldn't remember where from! Or a scrummy piece that has appeared from the stash that you just can't remember where, why, who, or what about!

Nothing in my *(somewhat sizeable)* stash, so I took all the bits of my quilt-to-be to the local fabric shop, just as well I work there....... having said that, you'll see that it had trips to several shops and a quilt show in the end!

94

Even the white of the table seemed better than the original mottled green. Having said that, there's no way I can work with lot's of white, I'm just too mucky! Anyhow .... if you're very nice to the people in the fabric shop, they let you try things on top of different fabrics........

....and even then I wasn't happy!!!

But see how the different colours affect the overall appearance of the flowers on the quilt? I was able to decide that I preferred a dark background, black would be too dark though. I did however remember seeing in the past a very jolly dark purple and black mottled fabric that would do the job very well indeed, if only I could find it again!! I did find some, it took me several weeks and a few swear words, but I got the last bit on a bolt at the quilt show in Exeter.

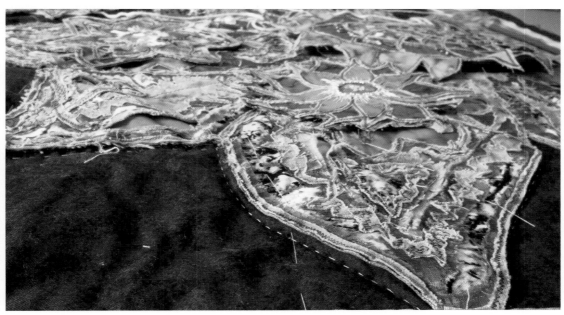

Having finally purchased my desired fabric, I have to admit to moving a couple of the smaller flowers about, evicting one completely from the quilt and replacing it with several extra small clematis-type flowers! I think all the placing of bits of quilt on top of different fabrics was to blame, the more fabrics I tried, the more things got moved about and seemed to grow on me. A classic example of an 'On-going Design' I feel!

Having appliquéed all the main bits of the design onto the new background, it was time to decide how to quilt it, if to quilt it, basically what to do with it even!! I don't particularly enjoy quilting. It is however, something that serves a huge purpose, it may be colourful, it is an integral part of the structure and design, therefore I can play with it!! *(but if it is meant to be small even stitching I rarely enjoy the actual doing of it!)*

So with this in mind, you will see how my version of quilting isn't quite the normal. *(no real surprise there then!)* I have shadow quilted the main body of the quilt using hand quilting thread doubled, (two different colours) in a fairly large stitch.

The background quilting is actually a large chain-stitch, using all six threads of a bright, variegated embroidery thread. This has hopefully made a colourful feature of the stitching resembling a vine.

I marked out the vine quilting design by dropping lengths of wool along the length of the quilt from above. The sewing line was then transferred onto the fabric using a white pastel pencil, which is very soft and easily removed.

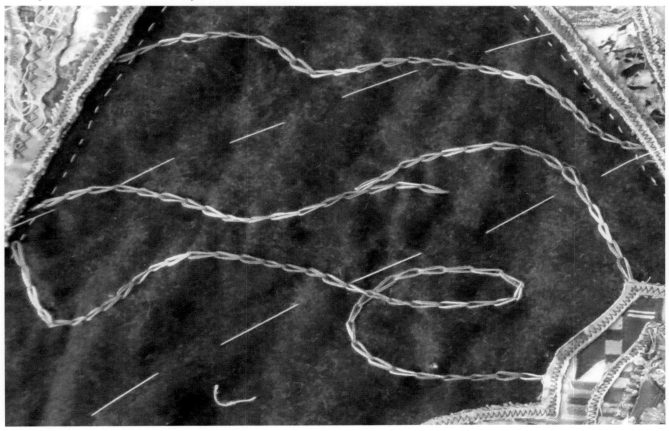

Dare to be different!! Get out the old dog-eared pamphlet of embroidery stitches if you've forgotten them and have a practice before hand. Any stitch that goes through all the layers of the quilt will do the job! A quilt is a three layered item held together with some form of stitching through all layers.

I can remember chain stitch was the very first fancy stitch I learned in school, followed closely by blanket stitch, I wonder if that still happens?

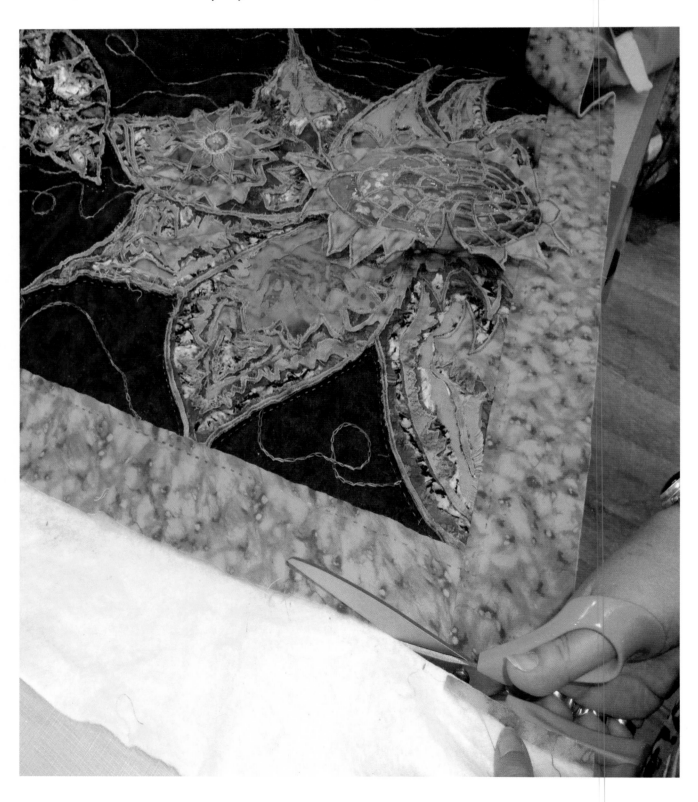

The quilting is finished, you can also see how the centre of the main flowers are raised from the surface of the quilt.

Finished!!

(That's Padstow in the background in case anybody is interested.)

The Gallery.............

I've been playing with this technique for many years now. I've built up a bit of a collection of finished items which I thought might be fun, if not useful, for you to see.

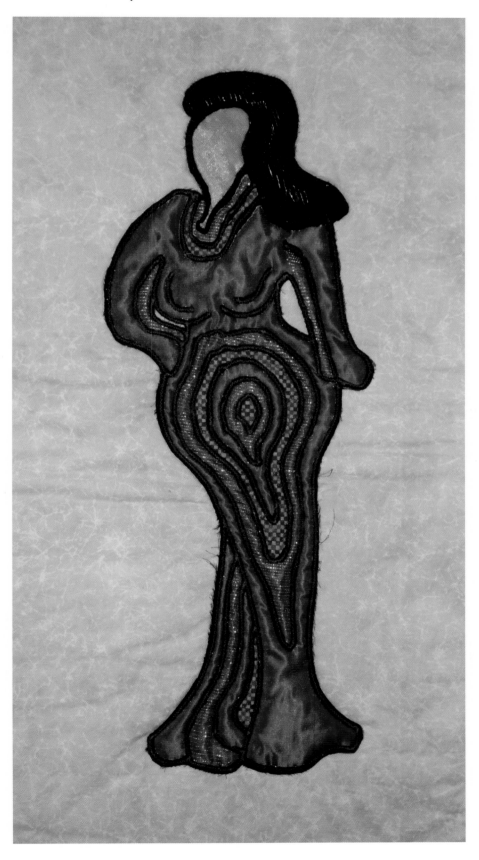

'Harvey'

'Work in progress.....'

I've left this one as it is, just because I like it that way!!

'The Owl'.......(who lost the pussy cat??)

'Sunflowers'!

'Circles'

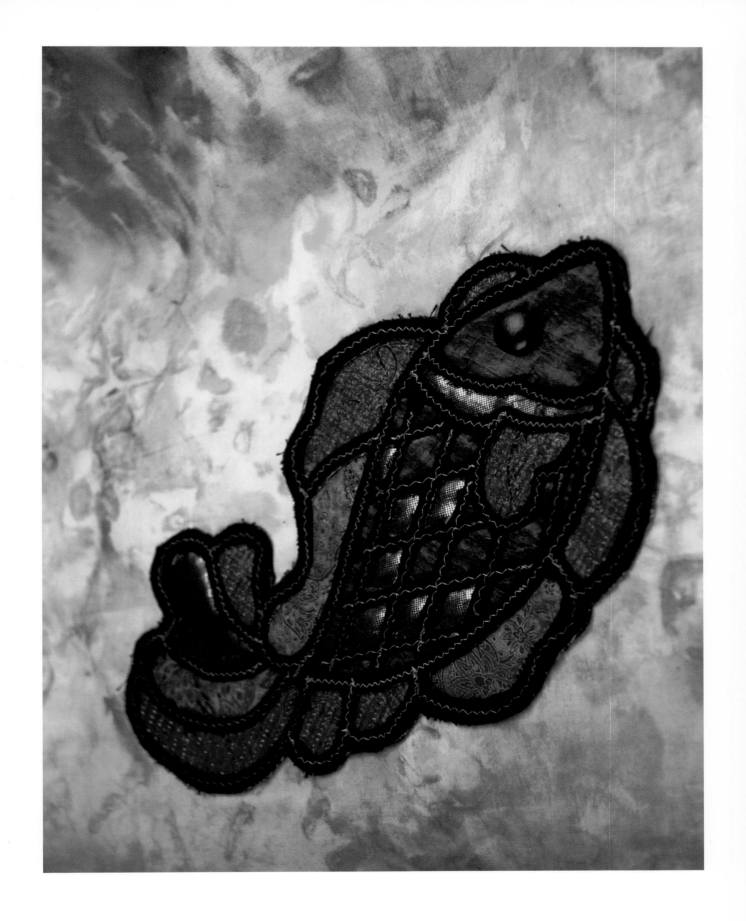

'Fishey-ness'

'Snail-pot'

'Straight Curves'

'A whole Heap Of Flowers'

'Buggy'

'Snails'!!

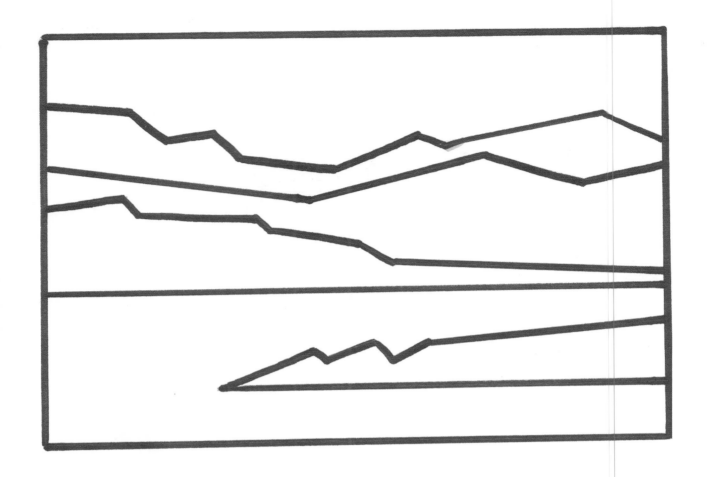

118

119

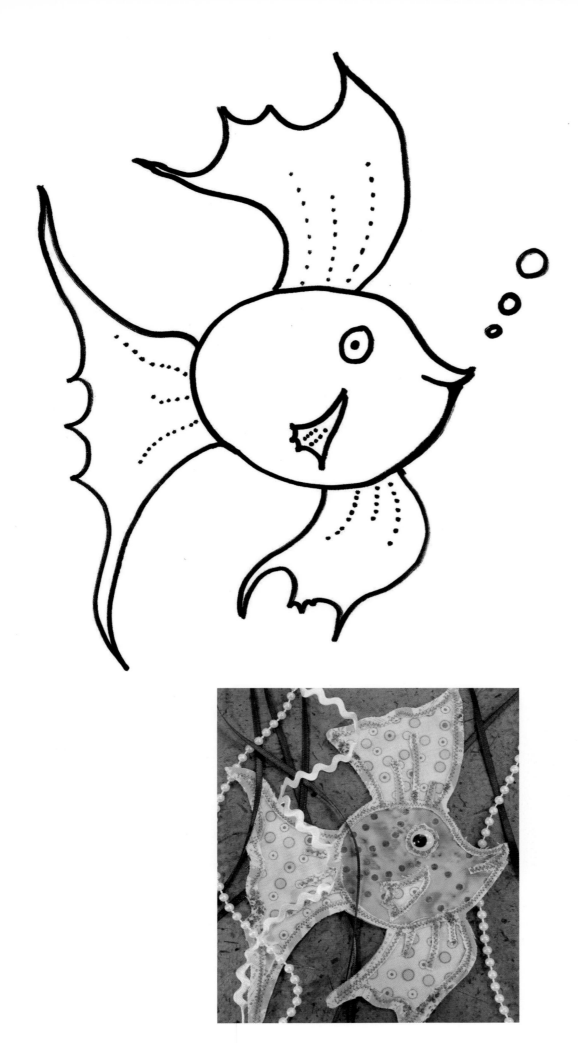

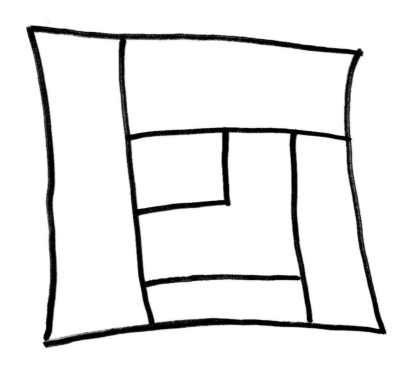

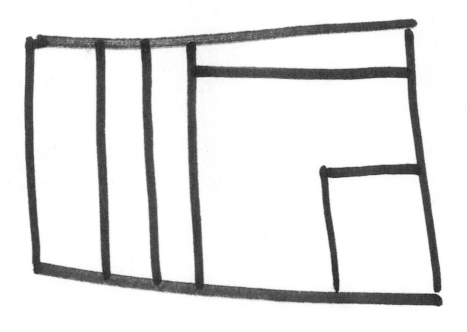

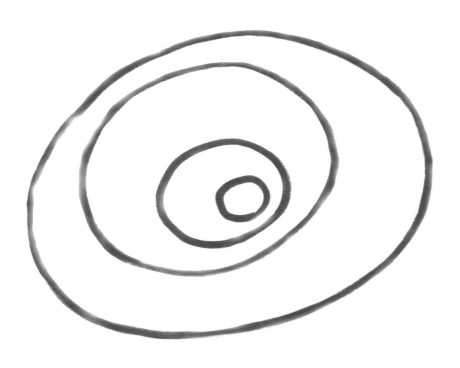

124

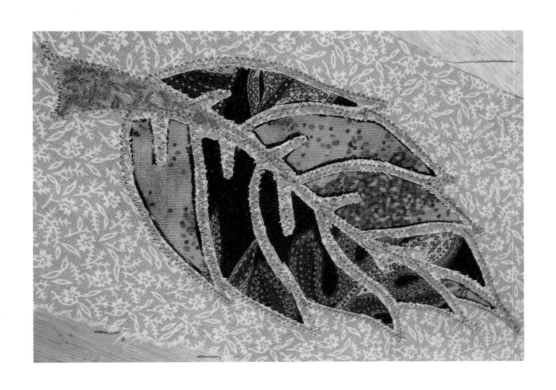

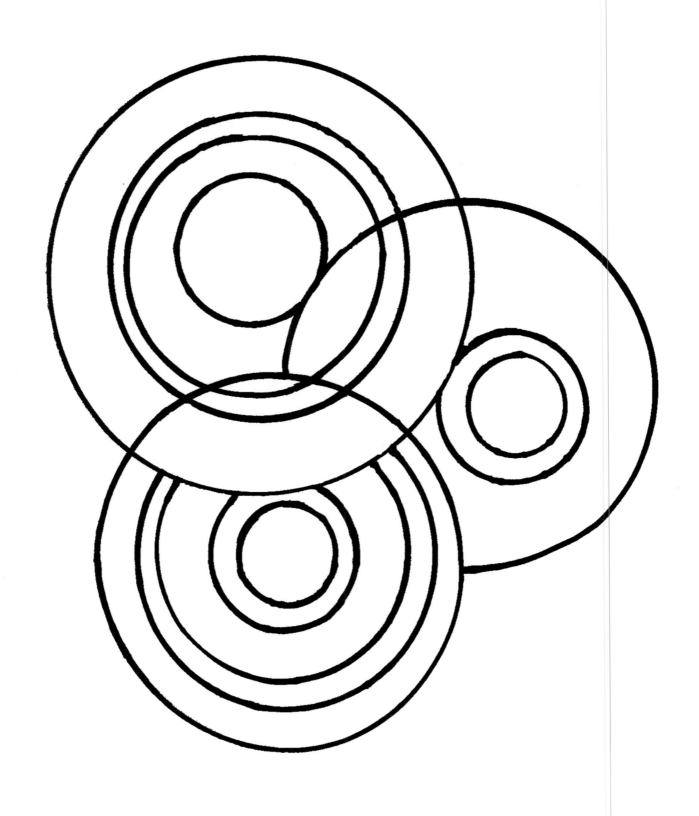

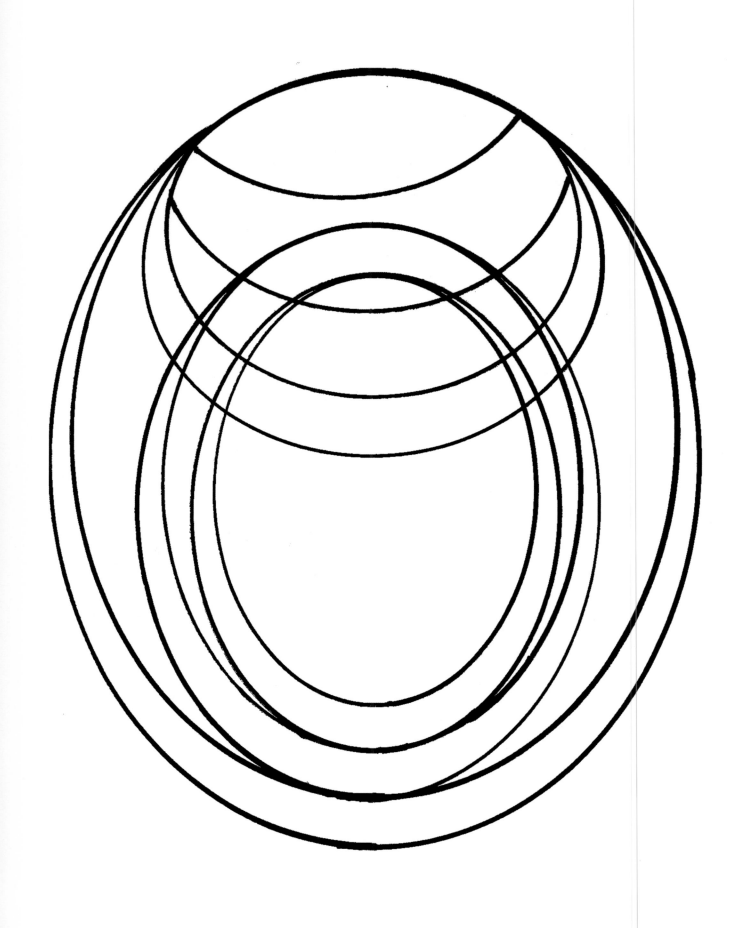

130

132

133

Meet the author......

I'm Abbie Searle, also known as Abbieanne. I patchwork and quilt. I paint and I play.
I manipulate fabrics and ask you to use your own imagination.

I teach and encourage others. I love colour and fabric. I like to laugh. I'm also very nosey...

I've always loved anything to do with art, the bigger, brighter and more tactile the better.
I found patchwork and quilting over a decade ago when I was on an economy mission to
make a quilt for a present. I saw one in a shop, didn't like the colours and decided I could
do that…... well, that's when the obsession started….....

I could fill pages with guff about what I do, but I would prefer it if you look at my work
and make up your own minds. I will say that the obsession led me into getting some C&G
qualifications in Design, Patchwork & Quilting and Embroidery, these on top of my art
qualifications and many years of just messing about in any artistic material or medium
I could afford at the time!

I teach textile art, patchwork & quilting classes. I teach requested craft workshops in a
range of techniques, not just fabrics. I trundle my quilts, some by me, some not, around
to group meetings and stand talking at people about them, local WI's are getting to know
me well! I have a wonderful time meeting people and hopefully inspiring them to do a bit
themselves.

I'm also extremely lucky to find myself living
in picturesque North Cornwall.